LIVING WITH ANGELS

God's Protection for His Children

Theodore W. Fornof,
Captain AUS (Ret.)
BC-HIS

PRESS

This Book is dedicated to my children, who I love very much, Kenneth, Richard, Patricia and Debi. I am sorry I had to be away so much and had to leave you in the loving capable hands of your mother, Marilyn, who is waiting for us in Heaven with Richard. I am proud of each of you and I am looking forward to all of us being together again for a joyful reunion in Glory.

Walking under the Shadow of the Almighty through life has been an adventure beyond my wildest expectations. I would have been killed, many times over, had it not been for the protection of my loving Heavenly Father.

I Praise His Holy Name and thank Him for Psalm 91 and His promised protection.

Psalm 91:1-16 .1) He that dwelleth in the secret place of the most High shall abide under the shadow of the Almighty. 2) I will say of the Lord, He is my refuge and my fortress: my God: in Him will I trust. 3) Surly he shall deliver thee from the snare of the fowler, and from the noisome pestilence. 4) He shall cover thee with his feathers, and under his wings shalt thou trust: his truth shall be thy shield and buckler. 5) Thou shalt not be afraid for the terror by night; nor for the arrow that flieth by day; 6) Nor for the pestilence that walketh in darkness; nor for the destruction that wasteth at noonday.7) A thousand shall fall at thy side and ten thousand at thy right hand; but it shall not come nigh thee. 8) Only with thine eyes shalt thou behold and see the reward of the wicked. 9) Because thou hast made the Lord, which is my refuge, even the most High, thy habitation; 10) There shall no evil befall thee, neither shall any plague come near thy dwelling. 11) For he shall give his angels charge over thee, to keep thee in all thy ways. 12) They shall bear thee up in their hands, lest thou dash thy foot against a stone. 13) Thou shalt tread upon the lion and adder; the young lion and the dragon shalt thou trample under feet. 14) Because he hath set his love upon me, therefore will I deliver him; I will set him on high, because he hath known my name. 15) He shall call upon me and I will answer him: I will be with him in trouble; I will deliver him, and honour him. 16) With long life will I satisfy him and shew him my salvation.

Contents

Preface

As I relive the events of my earlier life, my life seems like a big dream. Many of these events came sharply to my mind. Others came to life over time, as the Holy Spirit in my mind renewed them. He reminds me of the many works He had performed for me, and my family. If it were not for Him neither I, nor my family would be here today.

I write of these adventures not to brag on me, but to show you doubters of the Christian walk, that there is a definite advantage to walking close to the Almighty God and His Son, Jesus. Jesus said He would never leave us or forsake us. His Children can trust in this advantage. This is why I am here. To tell you of the greatest things that has happened to me. In addition, I am still alive to tell you of it.

You too can live in this protection. Turn your life over to Jesus and live in His protection. You do not have to wait until death takes you to your destination, you can enjoy it now.

Introduction

I was raised in a Christian home. I was saved at a very young age. We attended a church where every time you sinned, you had to be saved over again. I have been saved about a hundred times, it seems, so I do not know which one took. World War II broke out when I was in High School. I knew I was going to be drafted, so I left High school in my Jr. Year to see the country I was going to fight for. My cousin Chuck and I took a 1933 Plymouth sedan and set out to see the country.

Gasoline was rationed, and all we had was an "A" Coupon Ration book, which was only the basic minimum gas allowance. We would buy gas out of the Service Station's shrinkage allowance. As we traveled. our car's gas gauge was broken, so it always read empty. We would travel until we ran out of money and then stop and get a job. Jobs were plentiful because so many men had gone into the service. When we had saved up enough money, we took off again. We worked in restaurants, Construction sites for the Army, and in Hotels. We returned home on Christmas Eve, 1943, and we were soon drafted into the Army.

After retiring from the Army, I owned a Hearing Aid business for 20 years. I was licensed in Washington and Oregon. I was Board Certified in Hearing Instrument Sciences, BC-HIS. I traveled all over Washington and Oregon testing hearing, selling, fitting, and servicing hearing aids.

This book is about a lifetime of protection while walking close to the only Son of the Living God, Jesus.

Chapter 1

My Youth

Hiding Behind a Couch.

I was born, Feb. 25, 1926 into a Christian home in Oil City, PA. My mother's family was in the Salvation Army and their family played their instruments on street corners and preached. My Mother and Father held Bible studies in our home. My earliest memories are of sneaking into the living room and hiding behind the couch and listening to the Bible studies. I must have been only a year or so old.

First Grade:

Prayer on Walk to School.

In my First Grade in school, I had to walk about a mile to school. On the way, I had to cross a dangerous area on a curve in the road at a dip that caused a number of accidents. The cars would enter the hidden curve too fast at the dip and hit the front of the grocery store I had to pass. My mother taught me how to pray for protection as I walked to school. I used this teaching as a basis for prayer throughout my life.

Union Goons

My Dad was in the automobile business. I worked part time sweeping and cleaning up. One night I was helping him on a repair job. I was tightening bolts for him and I broke one off. I learned that things have a breaking point. He sold Plymouth and Desoto Automobiles. He would buy his cars from the Detroit factory and have them shipped by ship to Cleveland Ohio where he would take a carload of drivers over and drive them back home to Oil City, PA. Sometimes he would take me with him. I was always happy to skip school and go with him. This was during the 1930's depression.

We were on another trip. There had been Union trouble but it seemed to have calmed down and it seemed to be safe for me to go along. The union was trying to take over the car transport business. You see them all over the highways today hauling big loads of new cars. This was just the introductory period and things got nasty. I was about to be introduced to the real world. I was probably in the fourth grade in school. Things went fine until we got to Cleveland. When we got to town the Port went on strike.

Dad went to City Hall for a permit to carry a concealed weapon. They denied him so he went around carrying his pistol in his hand. We were stopped by a union mob. A big guy called the "Goon" came up to dad's window and told him they were going to beat me up and throw me into the lake as they had done to another dealer's son the week before. Dad stuck his pistol in the Goon's face and told him that if he touched me, he was going to look like a sieve. The Goon backed off and let us go, but it was not over yet. We headed down to the docks to pick up our cars. Near the docks, the road passed under a Railroad Overpass. When we got there, the road was blocked solid by a union mob.

Dad threw the car into second gear and floor boarded it. He laid on the horn and headed straight at the center of the mob blocking the road. There were also men on top of the overpass throwing stuff onto the road below. When dad got to the mob, they scattered. What we then discovered was that right at the other side of the underpass the road took a sudden 90-degree turn to the left. We took that turn on two wheels. When we arrived at the docks, all activity had stopped. Cars, being driven up the ramps onto the car carriers, were parked on the ramps and brakes locked. We went into the office and the haggling started. The union said there was no way Dad was going to drive those cars out of here. Dad said those cars were his, bought and paid for and he would take them home anyway he wanted to. It was deadlocked.

About 11, PM Dad received a phone call from his brother Carl back in Oil City, PA. Uncle Carl told Dad to put the Union guy on the phone extension. He wanted them to get this message. Uncle Carl went on to say that he had seven carloads of National Guardsmen armed with Baseball bats and everything they could get their hands on. They were ready to come to town and clean house if those cars were not released, NOW! We drove those cars home that night.

The factory then shipped Dad his years' supply of cars all at once instead of spacing them out over the year. It was depression time and no one could pay for the cars that they had purchased, let alone pay for a new car. The cars, were parked, all over town, and were being ticketed by the police. He sent them all back to the factory and stopped selling cars. Dad lost his business, and everything. Dad ended up going to work making torpedoes for the war.

Hot Wiring

Our Home

Mom had a nervous breakdown in all of this. We moved way out into the country into a farmhouse with 15 rooms. It had no electricity but piped natural gas lighting throughout the house in each room. Dad got a job in another town so we moved from the fifteen-room house into a 9-room house. Then Dad changed jobs again to making torpedoes and we moved from the nine room house into a new One room unfinished house. It was nothing but a shell. It had no partitions, and completely bare insides. I had to dig a well for water, and I had to dig the hole for the Out House. Dad had one light wired in and inspected to get the electricity turned on.

We then put up the partitions for the rooms and Dad taught me how to wire electricity. I then proceeded to wire the house. The only problem was that Mom wanted to use the iron while I was wiring the house. I learned to "Hot Wire." In learning to hot wire, I melted the screwdriver tip when I shorted it out. The melted blob on the screwdriver blade was so tough that it ruined the file I used to try to make the screwdriver useful again. I gave up. That melted blob was too tough for anything I had. That wiring experience I had was to be of great help to me later in life.

Waterfall Photo
in Yellowstone Park

During WW II, they were drafting 18 year olds into the Service. When I was 17, I knew I would be going into the Service. I decided I wanted to see the country I would be fighting for. My cousin, Chuck, and I decided to tour the country. He was a year younger then I. During this tour, we visited Yellowstone National Park in Wyoming. We came across a beautiful Water Fall that I wanted to take a picture of. There was a tree in the way so I stepped over the guardrail to get a better view. I stepped onto gravel and it gave away.

I slid down the embankment of the canyon wall. About 50 feet down there was a little nubbin sticking out of the canyon wall. I managed to get stopped on it. I took the picture, stuck the camera strap in my mouth and scampered back up that slippery canyon wall to safety. Thank you

Lord Jesus. He had to of helped me back up that slippery canyon wall.

South Carolina

Car Hit Bridge,

Lost Brakes

We were traveling in a 1933 Plymouth sedan. Dad had put a metal roof on it and that is where we normally slept. We would shut the doors on the blankets like a big sleeping bag that was better than sleeping on the ground with the bugs. If the weather did not permit, we would sleep inside the car. Everything we owned we carried in the backseat of the car. The backseat area was full to the top of the front seat back.

Somewhere in South Carolina, I was sleeping in the back seat while my cousin, Chuck, was driving. He missed a turn in town and went out a back road. It came up on an unexpected "T" turn at a river and he was going too fast. He made the turn but at that speed, he was hanging onto the riverbank along side of the road. Before he could get the car stopped, he hit the bridge at the intersection of another road. We hung on the riverbank with just enough ice on the river to keep us from rolling over into 8 feet of water.

Help arrived and got us back onto the roadway. I had to drive. Chuck had been pushed into the steering wheel by the impact. The steering wheel was bent to fit his body. When we hit the abutment my weight in the backseat had sprung the seat forward and bent the seat to where the seat had to be pushed back to make room to turn the steering wheel, where it was bent to fit his body. I drove the car forward and it stopped. I drove the car backwards and it stopped. I picked the front bumper up off the ground with its' two fog lights and put it on the backseat. Three of the other four headlights were broken off so we only had one headlight left... Everything else seemed to work so we took off.

It was night and I found the road we wanted to take. It led us to a ferry to take us over the bay. The ferry was just coming in and there was no one ahead of us waiting. I put the brakes on but nothing happened. We had lost our brakes. I found out later that when we hit the bridge, the radiator had been shoved back close enough to the engine that it cut the hydraulic brake line on the flywheel, causing a loss of brake fluid. I did a fast "U" turn.

OK here is the situation with the car. It was a 10 year old worn out Plymouth. The transmission was worn to where it jumps out of gear. That model had an innovation that we do not have now. It was called: "Free Wheeling." In the Free Wheeling mode it goes into neutral every time you took you let off on the gas pedal. That caused us to break an axle in Death Valley, CA.

When driving the car that meant to stop I would have to double clutch the transmission into Low Gear, grab the Free Wheeling control with my left hand to keep it from jumping out of gear, turn the engine off, and grab the gear-shift with my right hand to keep the transmission from jumping out of gear into neutral. Then I would have to brace my feet on the floorboard to push the seat back far enough to turn the bent steering wheel with my stomach. I drove the car like that up the east coast, went sight-seeing in Washington, D.C. Then across the Appalachian Mountains, through Pittsburg, PA and about 80 miles north to home. We arrived there Christmas eve.

While crossing the Appalachian Mountains, on the downhill side of a mountain, the roadway suddenly turned into a beautiful highway. I relaxed and got careless. I let the engine slip out of gear into neutral. Without the car in gear to keep the engine running, the engine stalled. It was so nice I did not try to restart the engine. Going down the mountain the car picked up speed to about 60-70 mph, out of gear and the engine off. Down the hill ahead, I saw a red light. I thought it must be a truck in trouble. When we approached the light, our last headlight revealed a sign that read "BRIDGE OUT". I thought, "Gee when we crash that barricade we will lose our last headlight and will not be able to see where we are falling." At the last instant, I saw a little detour off to the right of the barricade. I took that turn on two wheels and found us on a gravel road, which ran parallel to the canyon the bridge went over. Because of the slippery gravel road, it must have been about a mile before I could get the engine restarted and the car under control.

We then traveled on across the Appalachian Mountains into PA, went through Pittsburg and about 80 miles North to our homes. The trip lasted 6 months, 33 states, and

18,000 miles. I think our Angels were glad for the rest. Praise the Lord. They worked hard for us on that trip.

Chapter Two

World War II

France: Fire in Tent

Shortly after returning home, I was drafted into the Army. I had Basic Training in the Coast Artillery, 40 mm Anti-Aircraft guns. Because of my electrical experience, I then went through training as a Telephone Lineman. About that time, the phase of the war changed from defensive to offensive, and the whole outfit transferred to the Infantry and we went through Infantry Basic Training. I then joined the 86th Infantry Division, The Black Hawks, as a Private. They were loading on trains for the invasion of Japan, for which they had special training. As the train was on the way to the ships, the Battle of the Bulge broke out in Belgium. The train turned around and we ended up in France.

After being followed by German U-Boat submarines while crossing the Atlantic Ocean, we stopped in Plymouth, England and then landed safely in Le Havre, France.

We stayed in eight man Squad tents at Camp Old Gold, France, while getting our equipment ready for combat. It was winter and cold. Our tents were heated by potbellied stoves, and we were given powdered coal to burn for heat. It would fall through the grates with no way to burn it. We cut #10 cans and made grates. It worked pretty well. My bunk bed was along the wall center, alongside the stove with my head at the stove.

One early morning one of the men came in from guard duty. He was half-frozen and wanted some heat. The fire had burned down. He picked up an open #10 topless can of gasoline and poured some gasoline on the coals to get the fire started again. There were some burning ashes in there and it caught the gasoline on fire. The fire shot up to the can he was holding and he dropped the burning can. The burning gasoline splashed all over the tent. I was awakened by his shouting and rolled over to look into the center of the fire. He was standing in the middle of it, stomping on it with his feet, trying to put out the fire. Our sleeping bags were the "Mummy" type. It was like a cocoon with a hole for the face. It was easy to turn over and not take your face hole with you. The opening zipper was at the face hole. If you turned over and did not take your face hole with you, it was difficult to find your way out of the bag. Luckily, I had my face hole with me where I could grab the quick release zipper to get out. I jumped out of bed grabbed my blankets and started to throw them on the fire to smother it. The other men then started to do the same. The fire was soon out. We could all have burned to death in that burning tent if the Lord's Angels had not been there. Thank you Lord.

My Point of Combat Entry WW II Cologne

WWII

Germany:

Wire Team Killed

I became a Combat Infantryman on my 19th birthday. My High school chum had his birthday on the same day as mine. We passed out Life Saver candies on our way into combat. I went into combat as an Assistant Automatic Rifleman. That means I carried a heavy load of ammunition. Shortly after we went into combat the Unit's Telephone Line Team were all killed. Since I had been trained for that in the Coast Artillery, they put me on the new wire team. There were two of us plus a Jeep driver.

We worked in three teams out of Battalion Headquarters. We were each assigned to our own Company. I was assigned to "G" Company, 343rd Infantry Regiment, 86th Infantry Division. I was to keep telephone communications between Battalion HQ. and "G" Company, and everywhere "G" Company needed a telephone, including out to the Outposts next to the German Army.

For combat, we worked in three teams. One Team would go with the combat troops and lay out the wire as needed. One Team would go back and pick up any unused wire from the day before. The other Team would move with the Bn. HQ. and setup the communications center. The Teams rotated. Therefore, if a telephone line went out that night, the Team that had setup the communications center went out to fix it as they had the easiest job that day. I remember going out alone one dark night trying to follow a telephone line to locate the break in the line. I would hold the line in my hands while following it through fallen buildings and over the rubble trying to find the break. I did not know if a German soldier had cut the line and was sitting there waiting for me, or what.

I had to lay a telephone line out to a machinegun out-post one night. It was located on our side of a creek. As I laid out the wire, the wire reel seemed unusually noisy that night. I felt like that squeaking thing was waving a red lantern and shouting out, "Over here!, over here!" Actually, it was so bad that the machine gunner did not want to stop us and give away his position. We passed the German position for the same reason. When we came to the end of our wire, we knew we had gone too far, so we rewound the wire with the same results. We finally found him with great difficulty.

WWII:

Piano Wire Head Slicer

We would usually travel in our jeep with the windshield folded down onto the jeep hood to give us a greater field of fire when we needed it. The Germans knew this and had a trick they often used. They would string a length of piano wire across the roadway at the proper height to slice your head off. The Army installed angle-iron wire cutters on the front of the jeeps to cut the wires. They used different designs to cut the wire. Ours had a bend to break the wire instead of a wire cutter. It was supposed to break the wire instead of cutting it. After laying a telephone wire one night from "G" Company to Bn. HQ., we were returning down the same road when we hit one of those wires that had been strung since we had just passed. I was sitting on the back of the jeep, above the seat, riding shotgun when we hit it. Our cutter did not cut that tough wire; it just snapped it up into the air without breaking it. In addition, it came back down on top of my helmet and slid down the back of my helmet. If it had gone down the front of my helmet, I would have lost my head. Thanks to my angel, I was in the right position to stay alive.

WWII:

Pole Splintering

Laying telephone lines in combat on the front lines was not an easy job. They were temporary lines so we laid them on the ground wherever possible. We had to protect them from damage. Sometimes at intersections, they would be torn up by armored tanks, so intersections presented special problems. We would either have to go under the road through culverts or overhead on poles. Climbing poles in combat was always nerve wracking. Could I make it up the pole and back down without getting shot? The trouble with poles at roadways is that they came in pairs. one on each side of the road. Getting up and down the pole was great, but that was only half the job. There was still another pole to climb. We did not wear safety belts in combat. We would stand on top of the pole on one climbing gaff and wrap the other leg around the pole. I was standing on top of a pole one time and the pole splintered in front of my face. I pulled my gaff out of the pole and slid down the pole, riding my boots to the ground. Thank you Lord, for blowing that bullet off course.

HIS PROMISE: Hebrews 13:5
"...I will never leave thee, nor forsake thee.

The comforting thought I carried in my mind all through combat was the promise of Jesus that "HE WOULD NEVER LEAVE ME NOR FORSAKE ME." With that promise in my mind, I was comforted with peace of mind while doing my work. It kept me calm during some harrowing situations.

Even today, I have a WWII combat buddy, who I shared a tent with; he has nightmares about the fighting. The love of God fills my heart with the peace that passes all understanding. I have never been troubled with nightmares or bad dreams. I have had buddies on both sides of me shot, but the Lord has protected me.

I nearly killed my buddy one night. I came in off guard duty. It was cold. I lifted the flap on my side of the tent and threw my rifle down onto my bed. It was a foxhole type with the tent over it. I hit my buddy on the forehead with my rifle barrel when I threw it into my bed in the dark. He knew I would be half-frozen so he was sleeping in my side to warm it up for me. He never let me forget how I returned his kindness. He is the one with the nightmares.

WWII:

Top of Pole and 4.2 Mortar

One dark raining night I was standing on top of a pole tying on a telephone line. The pole was on the left side of a barn. On the right side of the barn, one of our tanks was shooting it out with a German tank somewhere out of my sight. Suddenly there was a loud explosion under me and a sheet of flame shot up past me, barely missing me, I shot down that pole and found out that a 4.2 Chemical Mortar Unit had moved in and set up under my pole. I did not hear them and they did not know I was above them. Their first shot barely missed me. Thank you Lord.

WW II

Road Block

One night we had to lay a telephone line between Bn. HQ. and "G" Company. The Jeep driver was told how to find "G" Company. It had been held up in combat by a road block. We had to leave the road we were on and cut up across a field up a hill onto another road. The road block was down the road to the left and our Company was to the right. It was always nerve racking to have to approach our Company on the front line from the enemy side. We did not want to get shot by our own guys, mistakenly thinking us to be to the enemy. We laid a few lines to out posts and then headed back to Bn. HQ.

We had to start out down the same road the road-block was on. In the dark, the driver missed the turnoff down the field, and we ran into the roadblock. I hurriedly unhooked the trailer from the Jeep and turned it around while the driver almost stripped the gears on the Jeep getting it turned around. I got the trailer hooked back up and we headed back up the road, still laying out the telephone wire..Thanks to the Lord, the Germans did not open fire on us. The next day there was a big battle at that roadblock.

WWII

Table Top

The work was so strenuous working day and night keeping up with all the changes that I had to get some sleep. I was in a bombed out building with rubble everywhere. I cleaned off a dining room table and went to sleep on top of the table. Later one of the men came in and woke me up. He said, "Come on, we have to get out of here. The Germans are shelling us again." Thank you, Lord, for getting me out in time. I was so exhausted and used to the noise that the shelling did not wake me up.

WWII:

Blown Out of Jeep

One night our wire team jeep joined a small convoy of about five other vehicles. We were last in line. We had no idea of where we were or where we were going. I was sitting up on the back as usual, riding shotgun. It was dark, there were never any lights in combat except for an occasional flare, which would temporarily light up the area.

We were lost behind enemy lines. We sat at an intersection while our leader tried to figure out which way to go. It was foggy and just turning dawn. There was an explosion on the left side of our jeep and I was blown out to the right side. My legs had gone to sleep from sitting on them so long. I landed on my knee and tore my kneecap loose.

It turned out that we had stopped on the road in line with a German Anti-Aircraft 88 mm gun, about 300 yards across a draw. The 88 fires a high-explosive shell and they fired it at anything that moved. Because of the fog, they missed us and the first round went into the mud alongside of our jeep. I rolled over into the ditch, which was about 10 inches deep. I could see the gun shooting up our vehicles. A later shot knocked a telephone pole down alongside where I was, concealing me from the gun crew. I laid there under fire for 2 hours before being rescued.

A nearby American unit heard the shooting and sent a patrol out to see what it was all about. They reported to their unit and brought up an Anti-Tank gun to a curve in the road. There they cut a tree limb off and their first round missed the 88, but it hit their ammunition pile, disabling the gun.

After the war when I returned home, my mother asked me what I was doing on that date. I checked a little note-book that I had and told her about being blown out of the jeep. She then said that was the time she was awakened in the night and told Dad that Ted was in trouble. They knelt by the bed and prayed for my safety for 2 hours. Then Mom told Dad, "Ted is OK now. We can go back to bed." Thank you Jesus, for praying parents.

WW II

On The Way to Japan.

After the war ended we were regrouping and getting ready for Japan. We were staying in houses. In the house across the street from us, one of the men was in the basement washing his clothes in gasoline. He stopped to take a break. He sat down and lit a cigarette. The house never looked the same again.

WW II

The 86th Infantry Division

The Blackhawks

The 86th Black Hawk, Infantry Division served in General Patton's Third Army. When the war ended in Germany, it was the first combat unit to be pulled out of Germany and sent for the invasion of Japan. While we were enroute', President Truman had the Atomic Bomb dropped on Japan, saving an expected million casualties. If he had not dropped the bomb, I probably would not be here today. Nor would any of my family be.

Chapter 3

Philippines

Sitting on Telephone Pole Cross Arm

Since the war was over and we no longer had to invade Japan, we ended up on Luzon in the Philippine Islands. We setup camp in a coconut grove and had to wear our helmets because of the falling coconuts. It took us over a week to be acclimated to the heat and the humidity. Later we relocated to an area above Manila. There was no electricity and candles were scarce. Someone stole an electric generator from another unit and I ran lines thru out the camp for lights. I put a light in each tent.

We had to run a 220 Volt line across the camp to Headquarters. We used a 2-pair cable. I had received a new man who was supposed to know electricity. He strung the cable. He was supposed to hook the two red wires together and the two white wires together. However, he hooked the red and white and the red and white together causing a direct short. He did get the ground wire correct. I had to go and troubleshoot the line to find and correct the problem. The existing telephone poles in the area were metal because of the termites. The poles had one-inch holes in their sides for climbing. However, all I had were wood pole-climbing gaffs, and when you stuck one in a steel pole hole, your legs went horizontal, sticking out of the pole sideways. It was very difficult climbing that pole.

When I got to the top of the pole, I found I could not work in that position. I had to climb out on the cross-arm and sit sidesaddle on the cross-arm with the wire running between my legs while I sat on it. There were no safety lines. I just sat up there in the sun with my bathing trunks and combat boots on. About the time, I got the wires apart and repairing the connection, the barber decided he wanted to cut some hair. He started up the generator. Now 110 Volts of electricity would knock you off the top of that pole, but I took 220 Volts. Only my angels kept me on top of that pole. I let out a yell. The Company Commander was walking by at that time and when he found out what had happened, he called a company formation. He told them the only person that could start the generator was the one who turned it off. I nearly met my maker that day. After that, I ran the Company Telephone Switchboard until I left for home. I studied Radio while on the switchboard.

Chapter 4

Alaska

Dutch Harbor,

Aleutian Islands

After I left the Philippines, I had a 30-day furlough, and then, I was assigned to Alaska. On the way, I was stationed in Fort Lawton, Seattle, WA while waiting for the ship.

I went to church one Sunday and I was invited home for dinner. This was common in wartime as the folks honored the Servicemen. While at dinner, she told me about her brother's girlfriend. He was off in the Navy somewhere. His girlfriend, Marilyn, called and said she was coming over to visit. After dinner, I helped her clean and dry the dinner dishes. Later I took her home on the city bus. I had dates lined up with three different girls that week because I did not want to get serious with anyone. However, I stood all those girls up and went with Marilyn every night that week. Marilyn and I were engaged for three weeks before we got married, and knew each other for three days before we became engaged. Four days after we were married, I shipped out for Dutch Harbor in the Aleutian Islands off Alaska, in the Bering Sea.

I was on Special Duty with the Navy as an electrician when I got to Dutch Harbor. I then transferred back to the Army on the outer island. Dutch Harbor is an island within an island. I became the Electrician, Power-Plant Operator and the Fire Chief. When that part of the island was closed out, I took over the AFRS Armed Forces Radio Station WXLC. I was the Program Director, Engineer, Disc Jockey and Janitor. I ran the entire station alone. At that time, an opening appeared in the Navy Housing and I applied for it.

I lived in the duplex for about a month while waiting for Marilyn to arrive. An oil stove heated the kitchen area. My coffeepot was a large porcelain pot with no insides to it. I filled it with water, added a handful of coffee grounds and boiled it. When I wanted a cup of coffee, I would add a cup of cold water to settle the grounds. Then I would pour out a cup of coffee. This way I never had to make more coffee as the pot never ran empty. I would pull the pot to the front of the stove to heat it and push it to the back of the stove to keep it warm while I was gone. An excellent system. My wife, Marilyn, went by ship from Seattle to Whittier, Alaska, and then by rail to Anchorage. She flew on a military cargo plane, sitting on a rope cargo seat, to Cold Bay in the Aleutians. She then took a Sea-going Tugboat, Sarsi, the 90 miles from Cold Bay to Dutch Harbor on the worst night possible. It was in a blinding snowstorm we could not even see the Tugboat until the tugboat pulled up to the dock in Dutch Harbor. I had borrowed the Lieutenants' jeep to pick her up.

I gathered up her luggage, which had been scattered all over the boat. She had been sick and was cold. We then loaded into the jeep, which is not the warmest thing in an arctic snowstorm. It had a thin plywood unheated cab. She was half-frozen. I started home. We had to cross the airstrip to get back to the main base and the housing area. It was dark, no lights other than the jeep headlights poking into the storm. We could not see but a few feet ahead of us. We were traveling in the storm blind, then it lifted enough that I saw a log laying to the right of us. I quickly stopped. I recognized that log. It was laying at the waters' edge on the seaplane ramp. A few more feet and we would have been the bay. I thank the Lord that He lifted the storm enough that I could see the log. Marilyn was very cold. I told her not to worry; I had some good hot coffee waiting for her on the stove at home.

We made it home and I gave her some of my good hot coffee. She nearly strangled on it. She washed the pot and spoiled the coffee. It and I had grown ripe together so I thought it was good. It was about the color of the pot.

The Sarsi, the Seagoing tug that dropped Marilyn off, headed back to San Francisco. On the way it hit a floating mine and sank. Thank you Lord, it was after Marilyn had gotten off.

I was running the Armed Forces Radio Station (WXLC) in Dutch Harbor when she arrived. I was located on the brow of a hill. I had to cross an open area, on that brow, of about 1/2 of a mile long, to get to the housing area. In

the Aleutians, there was what was called, the "Williwaw".
It was a one hundred mile an hour wind. The snow went
sideways. There were big drifts, but the area in between the
drifts was usually bare. I had to cross this hill brow on my
way home at night from the Radio Station. Often times the
wind was so strong I would have to craw on my stomach to
keep from being blown off the hill crest. I could not even
get up on my hands and knees or I would get blown over
and who knows how far I would go on that ice.

One morning Marilyn and I along with a couple of
friends climbed Ballyhoo Mountain there on the island
of Dutch Harbor. Jack Londan used to live up there while
writing his stories about the North. The snow had a crust on
it from the sun. If you stayed on top of the crust you were
OK. If you stepped too hard and broke through the crust,
you went through to your hip. *It was d*ifficult to get back
out and slow climbing. It was a long slow climb to the top,

but what a difference going back down. The crust made

an excellent slide. We would slide on one side until it felt

frozen and we would turn to the other side. It did not take

near as long coming back down as it did going up.

Chapter 5

Korea

Accidents Pursued Me

In Korea, I was assigned to the 8070th Engineers. We were headquartered in Teague. Our area of responsibility was about 3,000 square miles of Central Korea. Our Commanding Officer was Lt. Col. Long. I was his Administration Officer and my desk was pushed up against his. All the Officers had many additional duties in addition to their main duty. One of my additional duties was as the Labor Officer. I had to pay about 986 Korean workers every two weeks. These workers were scattered all over the three thousand square miles in Work Detachments. We had to maintain the roads and utilities, etc. I would take a squad of Korean soldier guards and go to the Bank of Korea and draw out their payroll. It would fill a 21/2 ton truck with duffle bags full of money. I would sign for it with my Korean Signature Chop. In Korea it was the death penalty to use someone else's' chop. It was a carved circular piece of ivory. About the size of your thumb.

The trouble was that it would take almost two weeks to make the rounds to pay them all by truck. It did not give me time to do me own work. I decided to go by plane instead of by truck to pay them. I used the two seated observation plane which worked out faster but not safer. It was dangerous to fly in the same sky as the Korean pilots who were just coming out of the Stone Age where they used oxcarts.

We were coming in for a landing at one airfield when our plane spun around on one wingtip. When I caught my breath I asked the pilot what happened? He showed me the Korean plane that had just cut in front of us as we were landing.

At another site, we had already touched down in our landing when our plane shot off to the side, off the runway. Again, a Korean pilot was landing head on to us on the same landing strip.

Korea:

Plane

in Snowstorm

On one of our trips, we had to cross the mountains to the west side of Korea to a small town where one of our detachments was located. We buzzed the town and the detachment. Soon we saw the vehicles heading for the landing strip. We landed and they soon arrived. I paid the men and then we headed home. In crossing the mountains in the small plane, we had to fly low enough to follow the river as a guide to stay between the snow covered mountains. Everything was going fine until an unexpected snowstorm hit us. It was so heavy that we could not see the river, the mountains, or our wingtips. We were flying blind. We could not turn around to go back because we were between the mountains, and we could not see to go ahead. That is where the angels took over and guided us through the storm and over the mountains. It was a miracle. Praise the Lord.

Korea:

Helicopter

Power Lines

When I arrived back from one of my trips, an officer got into the helicopter I had just gotten out of and they took off on their trip. They were past due on returning. Hours later we learned that a helicopter had flown into some High-Tension Electrical Power Lines and had burned up, killing them. I had just gotten out of the same helicopter. Thank you Lord

Korea:

Plane

Mountain Side.

After another one of my trips, the pilot was exhausted but he had to take another officer on a trip. He got in after I got out. We learned later that they were killed when they flew into the side of a mountain. Thank you, Lord, that it happened once again after I had gotten out. The pilot was a good friend of mine. We had done a lot of flying together.

Korea:

Helicopter Shot Down

Many times, I would have to fly in a helicopter instead of a plane. After another one of my missions in a helicopter, a Col. got in and they took off on their mission. Later we learned they had gotten off course and were shot down. Thank you Lord that once again, it happened after I had gotten out.

Chapter: 6

Germany

Hitler's Eagles Nest Retreat

I had my family with me in Germany from 1957 to 1960. For three years I would take my family, Marilyn, Kenneth, Richard, and Patty with me and we would tour Europe. (Marilyn died from a heart attack in 1992.) Debra was born, before we left, in Stuttgart, Germany. We camped thru 13 countries in Europe. I tried to pick all the small countries. I had a big 1955 Packard and I would put 5-5gallon cans of gasoline in the trunk because it was so far between Military Posts where I could get gasoline. That Packard had the automatic leveling system. With that entire load, it would just come back to level. It was a beautiful system and I liked it. On one of our trips, we went up to Hitler's Eagles Nest Retreat near Berchtesgaden in the Bavarian Alps.

I was about 6 miles from Berchtesgaden when the war ended in 1945.

I drove up as high to the Eagles Nest as the road permitted. Only busses go there today. It was a steep drive to about the six thousand foot level. After enjoying our sight-seeing, we started back down the mountain.

The road had sharp curves, one after another. Partway down the mountain, I started having brake trouble. They were not working very well. Then fear struck me. I realized how high up the mountain we still were and we were losing our brakes from overheating on all those curves.

The car tires were a new design, which was to reduce friction and give greater speed and mileage. The trouble with that narrow tread design it had little gripping power and squealed at every thought of a curve.

The drum brakes were gone. It was like stepping on greased lightening to step on the brakes. The car just seemed to go faster. I could not turn the engine off, as that would lock the steering wheel and that would have been an instant disaster. The tires were constantly screaming on the curves and the more they screamed the more Marilyn prayed. The kids did not know what was going on and they thought it was all fun. I was concerned about the 25 gallons of gasoline in the trunk. I was riding the horn, the car only kept going faster. Tires screaming, horn bowing, curves, tires screaming, horn blowing, curves, tires screaming, over, and over,. Soon, they all blended into one big dream.

I do not know how we got off that mountain. There were no brake-loss turnoffs. Nothing was working except the Angels. God was answering our prayers and we soon found ourselves off that mountain. We did not remember going through the town. Thank you Lord for saving my family.

Flight from Germany:
Flew 20-hour flight
in 5 days.

Upon our return to the US from Germany, we flew out of Rheine Main AFB in Frankfurt, Germany. We had a newborn baby, (Debra born in Stuttgart, Germany a few months earlier.) Marilyn and I had four children. Our plane took off without incident. Before we had gotten halfway to the Azores Islands, engine trouble developed and we had to return to France for repairs. We were put up in adequate quarters for the night. We had to get more distilled water for baby Debra. We learned with baby Patty, on our way to Germany, that changing water every time as we traveled caused diarrhea.

The next day we loaded on a different airplane and we took off. Well, almost. Before we got off the ground, the brakes came on and threw us up against the seat ahead of us. The take off was aborted, and we taxied back for another try to takeoff. Once again, the takeoff was aborted, and we taxied back for a third try to takeoff. I looked out the window as we tried to take off again. People were lined up to see if we were going to make it this time. Marilyn was about to get off and walk. This time we made it off the ground.

We made it all the way to the Azores before something needed repairs. They had to put us up for two nights again while the engines were rewired. After getting more distilled water we were happily on our way again, supposedly to New Jersey. However, the East Coast was fogbound and we were diverted to Gander, Newfoundland. They had two Atlantic routes, the Southern one through the Azores and the Northern one through Newfoundland. We made them both. This time when we landed, the number four engine would not come out of reverse.

We sat in the terminal all day while they worked on the plane. The four kids slept all day. Finally, they told us they were going to put us up for the night while they worked on the plane. I sent Kenneth and Richard out to get our bags off the plane and onto the bus. We lived out of the hand-bags under the seats all this time. Kenneth (about 13) came back and reported to us that our bags were all on the bus and Richard (about 7) was standing guard on the bus. We went out to the bus and it was gone. We went back to the Terminal Manager and he did not know where it had gone. He had to check to find out where it went.

They got a ride for us to where we were to stay. As we pulled up, there was Ricky standing with the baggage in the middle of the driveway. He had big tears streaming down his checks. He thought we were lost, but he stayed with the baggage as Kenneth had told him to do. Marilyn and I were exhausted from sitting up all day and constantly checking on our flight. The kids slept most of the day, and were ready to play. We had to locate more distilled water for Debi.

After two planes, three crews, and five days for a 20 hour flight, we finally made it back to New Jersey, USA. What a relief. Thank you Lord.

Chapter 7

GA: Army Maneuvers

Helicopter Overloaded.

Later I was the Supply Officer for an Engineer Combat Bn. We were a part of the Army training maneuvers taking place in Georgia, USA. I was also the purchasing agent for anything that was needed. I would be given a list of the supplies needed and I would take a helicopter to a nearby town to get the needed supplies. I took off one time in a small helicopter and headed for a town to purchase the needed supplies. We landed in the town square and I found the local hardware store. One of the items I had to purchase was a large reel of heavy rope. Normally I would put the supplies into the litter carrier on the right side, the passenger side. I would then get into the seat. This time, however, the cable reel was too large to fit in the litter carrier. The only thing to do was to tie the reel in the passenger seat where I was to sit. I had to ride in the litter. It was like being in a cocoon. I was strapped in and when they put the cover over me, I had only a small green window over my face. I could not see anything but sky from that position.

We took off and headed back to our area. Upon arriving there, I was being helped out of the litter basket when the Major walked by and asked the pilot how things went. The pilot replied, "OK, except I ran out of right rudder!" When we were alone I asked the pilot what he meant by "running out of right rudder?" He replied that we were overloaded on the right side, the side I was on, and he could not steer.

We went around in circles all the way back to camp. Thank

you, Lord, for a safe landing.

Chapter 8

Kentucky:

Combat Engineers

937th Engineer Group, Combat.

When I returned in 1960, from a tour of duty in Germany I was assigned to the 937th Engineer Group, Combat, at Ft. Campbell, KY. My duties required me to do a lot of traveling in the Jeep over areas where there were no roads. Eventually those rough rides tore my diaphragm apart and part of my stomach went up into my chest cavity. I had a Hiatal Hernia. It was painful.

The Doctors did not want to operate because of the high mortality rate at that time for that particular operation. Eventually my ability to function became so limited that they decided to operate. After the surgery, the Doctor came in and told me he had fixed the problem. He had taken an extra tuck so it would not tear again.

However, that started a new set of problems. The esophagus normally slides in the diaphragm. The extra tuck would not let it slide. Therefore, instead of it sliding, it pulled. As a result, the constant pulling on the diaphragm as I moved tenderized me all around the diaphragm where it was attached to the chest. Not only that, it set up a muscular imbalance in that when I swallowed food, the esophagus would go into spasms and block the food from going into the stomach. If I took a drink of water, it would go into my lungs instead of my stomach. In addition to the pain pills, I had to take a muscle relaxant to relax the esophagus spasms so I could eat.

I then spent a week in the Army Hospital at Fort Campbell where they ran all sorts of tests. I watched as they took x-ray movies as I ate, etc. After a week of this, they decided to send me to the Walter Reed Army Hospital in Washington, DC. I spent seven weeks there as they tried to solve it. During this time, they gave me SIX Aspirins every four hours. That started my ears to ring and they have never stopped. Even today, my ears constantly ring. If I take an aspirin, my ears ring like sirens.

After seven weeks of analysis they decided if they went in to correct those side effects, they would only set up other side effects. Since I was getting close to retirement, they decided to just give me a lifetime supply of pain pills and send me home. The trouble was that the pain pills did not help much.

The pain pills only took the edge off the pain. I was never pain-free. I had to maintain a high level of pain medication because, if I waited too long, the recovery was too slow. As a result, I was often overdosed and appeared drunk, as I could not remember when I had taken the pills last, and I did not want the dose to expire again.

Chapter 9

Retirement 1

After my retirement from the Army, the fun began. I had to move my family and household to my retirement location about two thousand miles away to Yakima, WA. This became very painful as the more I did the more intense the pain became. Moving household furniture around really increased the pain. We relocated several times in Yakima before we found a home to buy and settle down. It became extremely painful to move any part of my body. I was almost an invalid. Nothing helped.

We had been looking for a church home, but they all seemed so boring. One time my wife, Marilyn, came to me and told me they were having special services at her sister Gloria's church and wondered if I would like to try it. We had not tried that one yet so I agreed to go. The man was a fiery Evangelist (Bill Hartley) from England and I liked him. He was straight Bible.

At the end of his sermon, He asked if anyone was hurting to come down and he would lay his hands on him and pray for them. I was in so much pain and nothing else seemed to work, that I decided to see what would happen. I went down for prayer. I told the Lord I wanted everything He had for me. He laid his hands on me and prayed. I had an instantaneous healing. I have not had a pill for that pain since. That was in 1964, Praise the Lord. Not only that, but I received the Baptism of the Holy Spirit, and spoke in tongues. What a joy. It is the icing on the cake for

His children. I did not know what had happened to me but it was a joyous occasion. It is a powerful Blessing, I have enjoyed all these years.

In Acts 1:4 "And, being assembled together with them, commanded them that they should not depart from Jerusalem, but wait for the promise of the Father, which, saith he, ye have heard of me. 5. For John truly baptized with water; but ye shall be baptized with the Holy Ghost not many days hence."

Acts 2:4 "and they were all filled with the Holy Ghost and began to speak with other tongues as the Spirit gave them utterance."

A truly great gift, to His children. He warns against those who alter His word and deny the power of it.

This is a gift only to His Children. You must be saved to receive this blessing. It is the icing on the cake. The last thing Jesus told His disciples was in Mark 16:16 "He that believeth and is baptized shall be saved; but he that believeth not shall be damned." (16:17) "And these signs will follow them that believe: In My name shall they cast out devils; they shall speak with new tongues;"

Mark (16:18) "They shall take up serpents; and if they drink any deadly thing, it shall not hurt them; they shall lay hands on the sick; and they shall recover.(16:19) So after the Lord had spoken unto them, he was received up into heaven, and sat on the right hand of God."

Are you a believer? Do these signs follow you? You must obey His Commandments. Not one jot or title will pass away from His Word. It never changes. Rev. 22:14 Blessed are they that do His commandments, that they may have right to the tree of life, and may enter in through the gates into the city.

Kenneth's Tire

After I had settled down with my family, my oldest son Kenneth finally came of age to get a car. He bought an old (1950, I think) Packard with bald tires. Without us knowing it, he took off to Portland OR. A distance of 200 miles over the Cascade mountains. 400 miles roundtrip. Upon his return, he drove into our driveway and a bald tire blew out. All the tires were bald. We praise the Lord that the Angels kept that tire from blowing out in those mountain curves.

Driving Asleep

After I retired from the Army, I owned and operated a Hearing Aid business for 20 years. In those years, I traveled all over Central Washington to follow up on advertising leads. I was licensed in Washington and Oregon, and Board Certified in Hearing Instrument Sciences. I spent a lot of windshield time traveling to my next appointment. On one of my long days I was traveling late to get to my next assignment, I fell asleep while driving. I was awakened by a horn blowing. I was going off the road into the oncoming traffic. It turned out that the blowing horn was my own. My left thumb was pushing the horn button. I never used my left thumb for the horn; I always used my right thumb. My angel was pushing my left thumb on the horn to wake me up. Thank you Lord.

Portland Curve
Too Sharp and Too Fast

I was traveling on an unfamiliar part of the Portland Freeway one day on my way to my next appointment. As I rounded a blind sharp right curve, the exit I was looking for suddenly appeared on my right. I had not seen any sign for it and I was already passing it. I swerved instantly to the right, but it was too late. It was too sharp of a turn and I was going too fast. My big Dodge Monaco broke traction and started going sideways into the guardrail "V" between the two roads. Just as I was about to slam into that guardrail, which would have come through my drivers' door, My car was lifted up, and I floated around the guardrail and back down onto the exit road at the 20 mph exit speed. Thank you Lord. That would have been disastrous.

Lady Too Scared to Pray

I enjoyed my Hearing Aid Business. One year one of the Hearing Aid manufacturers was having a convention in Las Vegas, NV. We had to catch a plane out of Portland, OR. I was sitting next to a business woman and she was scared silly because of the storm we were about to take off in. She said, "I'm too scared to even pray!" I replied,

"That is the advantage of being prayed up!" We made the trip without incident.

Portland, OR:
Airplane Fog

On the way to the Portland airport there was dense fog at the airport. I had a couple of business men with me. There were acres and acres of parking. We parked some-where in the fog and headed for the lights.

On our return flight from Las Vegas, we had to go by way of Las Angeles. I was seated by a businessman who was a friend of mine. He was telling me how his wife was going to drive across the Portland area a long distance to pick him up at the airport. As we were approaching Portland, the pilot came on the speaker system and announced that the Portland airport was closed due to the heavy fog. We were going to overfly Portland and land in Seattle.

My friend was upset because his wife would drive through that fog to meet him and he would not be there. He fretted on and on. Finally, I asked him, "Do you really want to go into Portland?" He answered, "Yes! More than anything else." I said, "OK, I'll pray so we can go into Portland." I prayed to the Father in Jesus' Name and asked that a clearing through the fog be made for us. I spoke to the fog and told it to get out of the way in The Name of Jesus A little while later the pilot came back on the speaker system and announced that we were starting our descent into Portland. The fog had lifted enough so we could land there.

We landed in Portland and my friend said he would get our baggage while I went to get the car. I stepped out the terminal door and I was in deep fog. I had no idea where the car was as we were talking when we parked. I prayed to the Lord that He would show me where my car was. I started to walk into the fog and walked straight out to my car. By the time I got back to the terminal door, he had just arrived with our baggage. His wife arrived shortly there-after. Thank you Lord.

Chapter 10

Retirement 2

Naomi's Fall

One day I took my wife, Naomi (Sis) to the bank. (Marilyn had died from a heart attack years before. Right after I sold my Hearing Aid business.) The parking lot across the front of the bank was next to a cobblestone sidewalk. The end parking space was next to the sidewalk, which wrapped out alongside the parking space. I angle parked on the right end with the passenger side next to the sidewalk. I got out of the car and went around the front of the car to meet her. She stepped out of the car onto the parking level with her arms full of banking records. When she took her next step she miss-stepped and did not step up to the sidewalk level.

She tripped. I watched her fall, full length, face down onto the cobblestone sidewalk. I knew she was badly hurt as she fell face down with her glasses on. I expected to see her face cut up from her broken glasses and her face looking like hamburger from the cobblestones. I picked her up and her glasses were not broken, not even a scratch. Her face did not have a mark on it. Thank you Lord, for giving her a soft landing.

Apartment Keys

After my wife, Naomi (Sis), died from shingles, I was despondent. A Missionary friend of mine, who knew of my computer expertise (I had one of the first computers in town about 1978), told me there was a Lady (Charlotte) who was having computer troubles. She was new in town and had purchased a new computer. It never operated right. She had been back for help and she still had troubles with it. She had gone to church for help. Their Associate Pastor and his wife tried and could not help. My Missionary friend and his wife spent days with her and it still did not work right. He told me I needed a diversion and asked me to help.

I met her and she was all frustrated because she had spent so much time and money on it and it still did not work right. After analyzing it, we upgraded it for their best model. It still did not work right and their technicians could not make this one work right either. One afternoon about four pm, I got on my cell phone with their technicians. They kept transferring me from one place to another place trying to find someone with the answers. Finally, about 1 am I was talking with the top technician in Microsoft. He told me that that machine had a flaw. A program had to be un-installed and re-installed and that they had never been successfully able to do it.

Since Microsoft could not fix it, why was I wasting my time? We returned the computer for a refund, and then the trouble started again. We were shuffled around and around. They told us the refund would be credited to her in a few days. It was not. Their credit card company said they did not receive the information. We were standing there and watched the information as it was being faxed to them. We went around and around for weeks and never did get all her money back from them.

During this time, we spent a lot of time together. The computer sat on the dining room table in front of the window. The blinds were always open. She fixed meals for us or we might go to the pool. Onetime I had her down to my home for dinner. Her apartment door had a deadbolt. It had to be locked and unlocked with the key. Her car keys were on the same key ring with the apartment key. She locked her apartment door and we drove both cars to my home where we had dinner. After dinner, she could not find her car keys to go home.

We looked all through the house, my car, her car, everywhere we could think of. Finally, I told her I would take her home and get the Apartment Manager to open her door. The Apartment Manager was sympathetic. He opened the door for her and we walked into her apartment. There on her desk by the telephone were her keys. Her car had been with us. How could her car keys have gotten into the locked apartment? The only way they could have gotten into that locked apartment was for an angel to bring them in. Thank you Lord Jesus.

I finally found the cure for my depression. I married Charlotte. She and I went Sky Diving on my 80th birthday. Charlotte kicked her feet out to dance on the clouds at 10,000 feet and the wind caught one of her shoes. We do not know what part of the county it is in. I told her I did not know if I would take her Sky Diving again or not. I could not afford to keep buying her new shoes. I bought her a new different brand of computer and it works fine.

Sky Diving on Ted's 80th Birthday with Charlotte

Denver Trap

It was July 8, 2005; Charlotte and I were returning home in the car from being with Billye Brim at Prayer Mountain at Branson, MO. Charlotte was driving. We were on Interstate I-70 highway, heading west, into Denver, CO. It was a multi-lane, about 6 lanes loaded with 18-wheeler trucks moving along at 75-80 mph. On a large curve, I could see about a mile ahead and about a mile behind. It looked like solid 18 wheel trucks, bumper-to-bumper and fender-to-fender. We learned later they called this area "The Mouse Trap" because so many cars had been destroyed here. We were in the middle, boxed in with them on all sides. Suddenly there was a piece of road debris that appeared from under the truck ahead of us.

With the short distance, between us and the truck ahead, and at that speed there was no time or way to avoid it. The debris tore a chunk out of our right front tire. Normally that would cause the car to be all over the road. I thought, "How are we going to get across all those truck lanes?" We were trapped! We were too small, too close and too low for the truckers to see our turn signals. However, Praise the Lord, that tire blew and right after those thoughts, our car was picked up, by the angels, and lifted over all that truck traffic and set off onto the right burm doing about 15 mph.

No fighting truck traffic to change lanes! We then crawled

about 300 yards to an overpass where I could change the

tire in the shade.

Tire with hole ripped in it.

As I was opening the trunk to get to the spare tire, a

pickup truck pulled up behind us. A large friendly man got

out and asked us if we needed help. He said, "My mother

tells me that everyone I help adds 2 years to my life." He

joyfully changed the tire and then led us into Denver to get a new tire. He would not accept anything for his help. Thank you Lord, you not only took us out from that possible accident, but I believe you also sent us an angel in our time of need. It pays to be prayed up and to have a close relationship with God. He translated us out of an accident and sent an angel to help us. Praise His Holy Name.

Blewett Pass, WA
Car Mirror

It was Charlotte's birthday, Dec. 1, 2005. I was taking her to Leavenworth, WA to see the annual Christmas lighting ceremony of that Bavarian style, mountain village. We were traveling up Hwy US 97 in snow going over Blewett Pass. It was snowy. On the way up this mountain pass, I got behind a large truck on a long straight road on an upgrade. The road cleared of traffic and I decided to pass the truck. I got about halfway past the truck when an SUV appeared on the horizon. No problem, I had plenty of time to get past the truck. However, I could not get up enough speed on the slippery snow to get past him. When I got to about the truck cab, that SUV appeared, right in my face. We were about to have a head on collision. It was a two-lane highway and nowhere to go and no time to get there. There was the truck alongside me on the right side and the guardrail on my left side. We were about to hit head-on when I called out to Jesus, I cried out, "LORD HELP US!"

The Lord immediately answered me and He said "SWERVE RIGHT!" Swerve right? That seemed like a dumb thing to do as I was alongside that truck. Nevertheless, I did not hesitate, I immediately swerved to the right and that SUV sideswiped me. I looked and the mirror on the drivers' side was gone. I looked in the rear view mirror and the truck was behind me. The SUV did not stop so I kept on going.

When we got to the motel in Leavenworth, I got out examining the damage to our car. THERE WAS NONE! The mirror on my side of the car was gone, but there was not a scratch on our car from that SUV. That mirror only sticks out beyond the car about two inches. My angel protected the car but took the mirror so I would have evidence of His protection. Thank you Lord Jesus. That SUV had to be within inches of our car to knock off the mirror and not touch any other part of the car. The Lord allowed the mirror to be knocked off as a witness to His protection. See the photos here.

Miracle picture.
Missing mirror. No Dings.

Miracle Picture.
Closeness of Mirror to Car.

You can have God's protection like this when you walk pleasing and in obedience to the Lord. We claim Psalm 91 over our car and us when we travel. God's Word works when you work it!

Lost Earring Restored

While Charlotte and I were at the Billye Brim meetings in Branson, MO in 2007, the auditorium was about full with over 3,000 people. We were seated near the back. Before the meeting started, we got an opportunity to move down closer to the front. After we were seated, Charlotte commented that she had just lost one of her earrings. People all around were helping look for it. It was not found. We prayed over it. Three days later, it showed up in the middle of the Motel room. The room had been cleaned several times. Thank you Jesus.

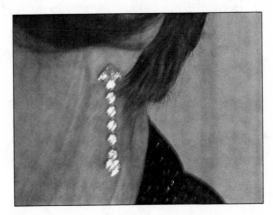

Lost Ear Ring Returned.

Are you ready?

Jesus is at the door!

Rev.3:11 "Behold I come quickly! Hold that fast to which thou hast, that no man take thy crown. (3:12) "Him that overcomes, will I make a pillar in the temple of my God..." (22:12) "And, behold, I come quickly; and my reward is with me, to give everyman according as his work shall be." Rev. 22:13 "I am Alpha and Omega, the beginning and the end, the first and the last."

Rev.(3:20 "Behold, I stand at the door, and knock. If any man hear my voice and open the door, I will come in to him and sup with him, and he with me.

God Loves You. John 3:16 tells us "For God so loved the world that He gave His only begotten Son, that whosoever believeth in him should not perish but have everlasting life." (3:17) For God sent not his Son into the world to condemn the world; but that the world through him might be saved. " (3:18) "He that believeth on him is not condemned: but he that believeth not is condemned already, because he hath not believed in the name of the only begotten Son of God.

First step is to get under God's Umbrella.

Romans 3:23 "For all have sinned and come short of the Glory of God."

Romans 10:9 "that if thou shalt confess with thy mouth the Lord Jesus and shalt believe in thine heart that God has raised Him from the dead, thou shalt be saved, (10:10) For with the heart man believeth unto righteousness; and with the mouth confession is made unto salvation."

1 John 2:1 "My little children, these things write I unto you, that ye sin not. And if any man sin, we have an advocate with the Father, Jesus Christ the righteous."

It is not enough to be just Saved, You have to walk an obedient and sinless life. Repent daily. We have an Advocate for us with God, Jesus Christ.

Most Christians know what they have been saved FROM, but few know what they have been saved TO. We Christians are in a war with Satan. You need God's power. It is available for His children for the asking.

Mark 16:17-18 And these signs follow them that believe: In My Name shall they cast out devils; they shall speak with new tongues; (16:18)"they shall take up serpents; and if they drink any deadly thing, it shall not hurt them; they shall lay hands on the sick, and they shall recover." We claim God's protection under Psalm 91 whenever we get into our car. This has been a glorious life with the Lord.

God has been good to us. He can Bless you also.

MY VISION OF CREATION

Ted Fornof

During my devotions one morning in Nov. 2005, I was talking with God about how all things were created. He showed me a giant Craft Hobby Shop in Heaven. It looked like a beautiful giant mall with many shops and Wings.

One Wing was for Agriculture, plants, flowers, trees, etc. Another Wing was for the Waters, fish, etc. Another Wing was for the Earth, minerals, etc. Another Wing was for the animals, etc. Another Wing was for the Air, birds, etc. There were many more Wings and shops. Angels do not just sit around in heaven twiddling their thumbs, God gives them something to do. Just like the artisans from on earth are practicing their craft in heaven building our new mansions.

God explained how He had a contest one time in heaven among the Creative Angels. He told each of them to create a different "Pair of a kind" Masterpiece of creation; Birds, flowers, fish, trees, plants, animals, minerals, etc. God set the guidelines for creation. In the Bird Wing for example, God had each angel create a different type of a bird. God did this for all the areas.

When the work was completed, God judged them and selected the ones He wanted. When God was ready Then He Said, "I have started Earth's creation. Go forth and install your handiwork on the earth!

One day almost a year later, my wife Charlotte and I were having lunch with a man from back east (Fred Harrison) who was attending the same seminars we were attending in Spokane, WA. The Lord had told him to stand on a certain corner and wait for a couple He was sending by, we were heading for a restaurant on our lunch break.

While we were eating together, I told him of my vision. He got all excited. He said the Lord had given him the same vision.

THIS WAS CONFIRMATION OF OUR VISIONS.